EXPLORING THE SUBATOMIC WORLD

Understanding
QUARKS

B. H. Fields
and Fred Bortz

Cavendish
Square

New York

To Brian, who has had to tolerate my quarky sense of humor all his life.

Published in 2016 by Cavendish Square Publishing, LLC
243 5th Avenue, Suite 136, New York, NY 10016

First Edition

Library of Congress Cataloging-in-Publication Data

Fields, B. H., author.
Understanding quarks / B.H. Fields and Fred Bortz.
pages cm — (Exploring the subatomic world)
Includes bibliographical references and index.
ISBN 978-1-50260-548-1 (hardcover) ISBN 978-1-50260-549-8 (ebook)
1. Quarks—Juvenile literature. 2. Particles (Nuclear physics)—Juvenile literature.
I. Bortz, Fred, 1944- author. II. Title. III. Series: Exploring the subatomic world.

QC793.5.Q252F54 2015
539.7'2167—dc23

2015007189

Editorial Director: David McNamara
Editor: Andrew Coddington
Copy Editor: Cynthia Roby
Art Director: Jeff Talbot
Designer: Stephanie Flecha
Senior Production Manager: Jennifer Ryder-Talbot
Production Editor: Renni Johnson
Photo Research: J8 Media

The photographs in this book are used by permission and through the courtesy of: SPL/ Getty Images, cover; MichaelTaylor/Shutterstock.com, throughout; ArSciMed/Science Source, 5; Sura Nualpradid/Shutterstock.com, 7; Thomas Forget, 7; Potapov Alexander/ Shutterstock.com, 9; Wellcome Library, London/Wellcome Images/An alchemist in his laboratory. Oil painting by a follower of David Teniers the younger. Oil By: David Teniers/ File:An alchemist in his laboratory. Wellcome L0051290.jpg/Wikimedia Commons, 10; SSPL/ Getty Image, 15; Public domain/File:Albert Einstein 1921 by F Schmutzer.jpg/Wikimedia Commons, 18; Hulton Archive/Getty Images, 19; Public domain, 20; Cavendish Laboratory, University of Cambridge; Supplied by The Public Catalogue Foundation/Wellcome Images/ File:Ernest Rutherford 1932.jpg/Wikimedia Commons, 22; Thomas Forget, 23; Burrell and Hardman, Liverpool, courtesy AIP Emilio Segre Visual Archives, gift of Lawrence Cranberg, 25; Jeff Kubina/File:Blacksmith working.jpg/Wikimedia Commons, 29; Thomas Forget, 30; SSPL/Getty Images, 33; © CERN, 34; Arthur Sasse/AFP/Getty Images, 37; Keystone/ Getty Images, 38; Lawrence Berkeley National Laboratory, courtesy AIP Emilio Segre Visual Archives, 39; Public domain/File:Diracb.jpg/Wikimedia Commons, 43; Science Source/ Getty Images, 44; Melirius/File:Murray Gell-Mann at Lection.jpg/Wikimedia Commons, 46; Thomas Forget, 47; Research Laboratory of Electronics/Greg Hren Photography, 49.

Printed in the United States of America

Contents

Introduction

This book is a scientific safari to the heart of matter. Its chapters trace the paths of many great philosophers and scientists who spoke first of **atoms**, then of particles within atoms, then of smaller particles that make up those particles. It describes how scientists have probed deeper and deeper into matter, always in search of something indivisible—not just subatomic but fundamental.

These pages will take you beyond **protons** and **neutrons**, which make up the **nucleus** of the atom and have their own books in this series. Those particles, at first thought to be indivisible, are made up of even smaller entities called "**quarks**." These oddly named particles can be detected within the subatomic particles which they combine to create, but they can never be set free. To the best of human knowledge, quarks, which make up one class of nature's fundamental building blocks, are always joined in pairs or triplets to form other particles, and can never be detected in isolation.

As you read this story of quarks, imagine being on an expedition through a jungle of mass and energy. Your task is to learn the terrain, to take in the sights, sounds, and the smells around you, and to become familiar with all forms of jungle life. If you are alert, you will notice small details hidden in a mass of observations. Those details reveal a pattern, a sign that quarks—and a great scientific adventure—lie ahead.

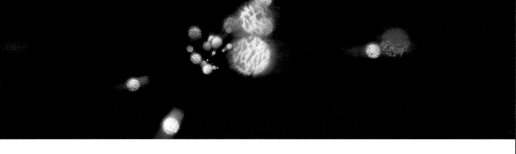

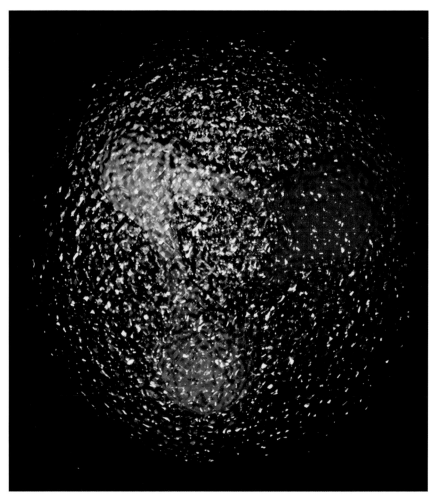

Exploring the subatomic world has produced many surprises. One of those is that protons and neutrons inside the nucleus of an atom are themselves made up of smaller particles known as quarks. This book is about that discovery and what it tells us about matter.

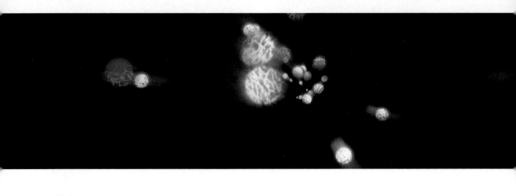

1 THE SEARCH
for the Fundamental

We begin with a question much older than science itself: What is the nature of matter? That question goes back at least twenty-five centuries to the Greek philosophers Leucippus and his student Democritus. In their time, scholars thought that they could understand the world through thinking alone. They imagined cutting a piece of matter into smaller and smaller pieces until it could no longer be cut. They called the smallest piece of matter *atomos*, Greek for indivisible, from which our modern word "atom" derives.

Though those ancient Greeks had no way to test their ideas, they decided that the properties of a substance probably depended on the shape and texture of its atoms. For instance, they suggested that water atoms were probably round and smooth, while atoms of rocks were most likely hard and sharp.

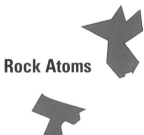

Rock Atoms

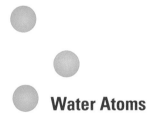

Water Atoms

Envisioning Atoms. Using thought alone, ancient Greek philosophers Leucippus and Democritus envisioned atoms as the smallest possible units of matter. In their view, different types of matter had atoms of different shapes and textures. For example, they thought that rock atoms were hard and rigid while water atoms were round and free flowing. Although they were incorrect in some respects, the idea of atoms has become the basis of our modern understanding of matter.

Later, science would require observations to answer such questions about nature, but the ancient philosophers were satisfied to answer that question with their minds. Thanks to science, we know that they were on the right track, but they were very wrong about the details. There was much more to atoms than they could imagine. Restating the question more scientifically, does nature have fundamental particles from which all matter is built? If so, how can those basic building blocks lead to so many different kinds of matter, and how can one kind of matter change into another?

The Road to Chemistry

The idea of indivisible, fundamental particles is very productive even today. Yet for more than two thousands years, it was nearly forgotten. As Democritus's life was nearing its end, Greek philosophy entered a "golden era" in which Socrates, Aristotle, Plato, and other great thinkers used the power of logic to discover the "truth" about the natural world. When Aristotle described the fundamental makeup of matter, he spoke not of atoms but of four **elements** that, in differing combinations, comprised everything in the world: earth, air, fire, and water.

Aristotle was right about different substances being made of elements combined in different ways. But today we know that the number of natural elements is not four but about ninety, and humans have created more than twenty that are artificial. Democritus was correct that a piece of matter cannot be cut indefinitely into smaller pieces and still remain the same substance. However, since most substances are not single elements but **compounds** or mixtures of compounds, the smallest piece of such a substance is what we now call a **molecule**, a particular arrangement of different atoms joined together.

So what has become of Aristotle's four elements? Water is a compound, earth and air are mixtures containing both elements and compounds, and fire is a process that produces energy as atoms rearrange themselves into different compounds. Meanwhile the atom that Democritus spoke of—the smallest piece of a substance—is a molecule. It is not indivisible, but its

separate parts are no longer the same substance. They are atoms of the elements that make up the compound. And as you will read in the next chapter, they are not indivisible either.

The road from the ancient Greeks to today's scientific knowledge of matter is long and fascinating. For many years, people who were interested in matter took part in the chemical science called **alchemy**. They tried to transform certain substances into those that were more valuable, often by heating them together. For example, many alchemists spent years

Aristotle's Four Elements. The idea of atoms almost disappeared when a new Greek philosophy arose. Instead of speaking about atoms, Aristotle spoke of four elements—earth, air, fire, and water—that made up all matter.

An Alchemist at Work. This seventeenth-century oil painting shows an alchemist in his laboratory. Though never successful at turning lead into gold, alchemy produced an understanding of certain materials and processes and eventually led to the science of chemistry.

searching for ways to turn cheap metals, such as lead, into gold. We now know that quest was bound to fail. Gold is an element, and neither the methods of alchemy nor **chemistry** can change an atom of one kind into another.

Some alchemists became fraud artists, camouflaging their failures to turn lead into gold behind showmanship. But others succeeded in developing a rudimentary knowledge of matter. They sometimes produced useful results, such as methods for extracting metals from their ores. In the seventeenth century, when they applied scientific thinking to their work, alchemy gradually became chemistry. By the eighteenth century, chemists, performing careful measurements, studied the behavior of gases, the processes of combustion and corrosion, and the relationship between electricity and matter.

Finally, in the early years of the nineteenth century, English meteorologist John Dalton (1766–1844) connected the work of those chemists to the ancient idea of atoms. He began by studying the gases of the air, hoping his research would help him understand more about weather. He realized that atoms could explain not only the way gases behaved, but also chemical reactions.

In 1810, he published his ideas in a book called *A New System of Chemical Philosophy*. That book revolutionized the study of matter. In it, Dalton explained that each element is made of a particular kind of atom, and all of its atoms are identical to each other. Dalton also stated that atoms of different elements have different properties, including their weight. Atoms combine, always in definite proportions, to form molecules, which are the smallest units of compounds.

Dalton soon had determined the atomic weight of many elements. He set the atomic weight of hydrogen, the lightest element, to one unit, and based the **atomic weight** (or **atomic mass**, the term prefered by today's physicists) of other atoms on that. For example, water is a compound of one part hydrogen and eight parts oxygen by weight. Dalton assumed that a water molecule had one atom of each element and therefore set the atomic weight of oxygen at eight units. Later research showed that water molecules had two atoms of hydrogen and one of oxygen, so scientists corrected that result, setting the atomic weight of oxygen to sixteen.

Using Dalton's approach, chemists identified more compounds and the elements that composed them, and they gradually developed a table listing the atomic weights of each element. No one had detected individual atoms, but Dalton had given chemistry a new basic vocabulary based on elements and compounds, and atoms and molecules.

Mendeleyev's Great Discovery

By the end of the 1860s, scientists knew of sixty-three elements and could see hints of similarities and patterns among their properties. They knew their atomic weights, their melting or boiling points, their densities (how much each cubic centimeter weighs), the way they combined with other elements, and the properties of the compounds they formed. Still, no one had come up with a successful classification scheme until the work of Russian chemist Dmitry Ivanovich Mendeleyev (1834–1907), a professor at St. Petersburg University.

Mendeleyev was famous for his detailed knowledge of the elements and their properties. In early 1869, he made a set of cards, one for each element with a list of its known properties. He then arranged them from top to bottom in order of increasing atomic weight. At a certain point, he reached an element that reacted chemically in ways similar to the one at the top of the column. It had the same property that chemists called valence. So he started a new column to the right of the first one. Eventually, he had an array of rows and columns. The elements across each the row had the same valence.

In other words, going across the rows, he saw those other properties changing. But when the row ended, the properties of the next element went back to where the row

Mendeleyev and Valence

Mendeleyev was not the only chemist trying to find an arrangement that made sense of the growing number of elements. But he had a distinct advantage over the others. He was one of the first to determine the valence of numerous elements and a pioneer in recognizing its significance.

In 1859, ten years before he came up with the periodic table, the young Mendeleyev went to Paris to study thermodynamics with renowned chemist Henri-Victor Regnault (1810–1878). A few months later, he went to Heidelberg, Germany, to work on spectroscopy, the measurement and analysis of light produced by various substances. He performed this work in the laboratory of two prominent German chemists: Robert Bunsen (1811–1899), inventor of the Bunsen burner, and Gustave Kirchhoff (1824–1887). Unfortunately, Mendeleyev's moody and stubborn nature soon led him to argue with Bunsen. He stormed out of the laboratory and, at age twenty-five, decided to set up his own.

That laboratory was where Mendeleyev began to measure the valence of various elements and to appreciate its significance to chemical reactions. Some elements have a negative valence and others have a positive one. When they combine to form a compound, the total adds up to zero. For example an atom of sodium (chemical symbol Na), with a valence of +1, combines with an atom of chlorine (Cl), with valence -1, to form NaCl or sodium chloride—table salt—with a net valence of zero.

Mendeleyev's knowledge of valence helped him decide when to end a column of elements in his table and start a new one. The result was rows of elements in his periodic table (and columns in modern versions) that all had the same valence.

had begun. It was a pattern that repeated periodically, so Mendeleyev's arrangement came to be called the **periodic table of the elements.**

Modern periodic tables reverse the role of Mendeleyev's rows and columns, but the relationships he discovered are still valid. Columns of elements have the same valence and behave similarly in reactions. For example, the alkali metals—lithium, sodium, potassium, rubidium, and cesium—all fall into vertical alignment, as do the nonmetallic elements known as halogens—fluorine, chlorine, bromine, and iodine. Horizontally, the elements follow a pattern of increasing atomic weight, going from one valence

A Momentous Discovery

Mendelyev's greatest early success with the periodic table was recognizing where there were gaps that needed to be filled by additional research. In November 1875, French chemist Paul-Émile Lecoq de Boisbaudran (1838–1912) discovered a new element, now known as gallium, that filled in a gap in the group of metals that includes aluminum. But did that element have the right properties?

It took Lecoq de Boisbaudran about a year to measure its density. His result, 4.7 times as dense as water, did not agree with Mendeleyev's prediction of 5.9. Mendeleyev, suspecting an error in the Frenchman's procedure, wrote a long letter asking him to repeat the experiment. At first, Lecoq de Boisbaudran refused. But six months later, he repeated his measurement, and his result matched Mendeleyev's predicted value. It was the first of many great triumphs for Mendeleyev's periodic table, which cemented his reputation as a visionary in his field.

The Notes of a Visionary. This document shows Mendeleyev's handwritten original periodic table and the notations that explained his thinking behind its arrangement. Other chemists later found the elements that he had denoted as question marks or that filled the gaps on the rightmost column.

to the next, and then, when the original valence is reached, the pattern begins again.

The table had gaps, which Mendeleyev attributed to elements not yet discovered. Certain that they would be found, he boldly predicted their atomic weights and densities—and he was right! As those later discoveries matched Mendeleyev's predictions, the periodic table of the elements was established as one of the great ideas of chemistry.

Still, no one, not even Mendeleyev, could answer the most important question raised by his discovery. Why is it periodic? Finding the answer took more than sixty years of research. And the most surprising part of the solution was the discovery that atoms are not fundamental at all!

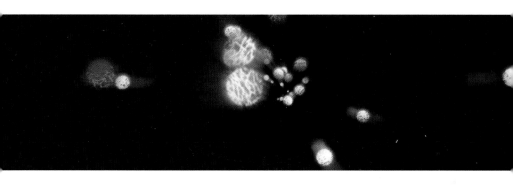

2 SMALLER
than Atoms

I n the years that followed Mendeleyev's publication of the periodic table, chemists around the world continued to discover new elements, gradually filling in the gaps in the table. Chemistry had become the science of atoms, and the periodic table was a road map to their properties. But many questions still swirled. Are elements really made of atoms? If so, what are those atoms really like? What makes each element so different? What makes elements in the same column of the table (or row in Mendeleyev's original table) so similar?

The Divisible Atom

As more elements were discovered, scientists began asking themselves how something as fundamental as atoms could be so complex. They wondered if atoms were more like compounds

The Reality of Atoms

As powerful an idea as the periodic table proved to be, it still did not persuade all scientists that atoms actually existed. Scientists are trained to be skeptical. Even when evidence showed that matter behaves as if it is made of atoms, some scientists required the direct detection of atoms or their effects before they could accept them as real.

Albert Einstein Lecturing in Vienna in 1921. In 1905, Einstein published three remarkable papers, including one that described his famous theory of relativity. Another explained that Brownian motion was the result of collisions between molecules in a fluid and bits of dust or pollen.

It turned out that scientists already had evidence for atoms, but they didn't recognize it. In 1905, a German-born Swiss patent clerk named Albert Einstein (1879–1955), who is most famous today for his **theory of relativity**, finally realized that evidence of atomic effects had been accumulating for nearly eighty years, beginning with an 1827 observation by English botanist Robert Brown (1773–1858). Through his microscope, Brown observed pollen grains suspended in water and noticed that they followed random jiggling paths. That phenomenon became known as **Brownian motion**.

As other scientists studied Brownian motion more carefully over many years, they accumulated detailed measurements of the paths of different sized particles at different temperatures. Einstein calculated the expected motion of dust or pollen particles bombarded by rapidly moving atoms or molecules in a fluid, and the results matched Brownian motion perfectly. Brownian motion didn't reveal individual atoms or molecules, but Einstein's calculations showed clearly that the movement of the pollen grains resulted from the combined effects of atomic collisions. That result removed the last scientific doubts of the existence of atoms.

Robert Brown, Discoverer of Brownian Motion. This engraving of a circa 1810 painting shows Brown when he was keeper of the Botanical Department at the British Museum. In 1827, he first observed the phenomenon that would become known as Brownian motion.

J. J. Thomson in 1908. Thomson was the first scientist to recognize that atoms were made up of smaller particles. In 1897, he realized that a beam he was studying was made of tiny, negatively charged particles that had less than a thousandth of the mass of hydrogen atoms. We now know those particles as electrons.

than elements, built up from a small set of fundamental subatomic particles that combined in particular ways.

The first firm evidence of particles smaller than atoms came from J. J. Thomson (1856–1940) of Cambridge University in England. In 1897, Thomson described the discovery of a tiny bit of matter that we now call the **electron**. It was less than a thousandth as heavy as the lightest known atom, hydrogen, yet it had as much negative electrical charge as that atom might carry in positive charge. By then, scientists knew that electricity was related to chemical reactions and valences, and thus it was probably important in atoms. Thomson's discovery suggested that atoms are composed of tiny negatively charged electrons and much heavier positively charged particles held together by electric forces.

The discovery of the electron led scientists to understand more about the periodic table of elements. Not only did the atoms increase in weight along the table's rows and columns, they also increased in number of electrons, each atom having one more than its predecessor. Each element could now be labeled by a distinct **atomic number**—its number of electrons—as well as by its weight. Thomson began to think about the inner details of atoms, especially the large ones with lots of electrons. Since electrons were so light compared with the much greater mass of the atoms, he proposed that an atom was like a plum pudding with tiny electrons plums scattered throughout an electrically positive mass. Other physicists imagined atoms differently, perhaps as tight clusters of positive and negative charges.

Many ideas seemed sensible, but which best represented nature? New Zealand–born Ernest Rutherford (1871–1937) had an idea about how to explore that question. As a student in Thomson's laboratory between 1895 and 1898, Rutherford was among the first to study **radioactivity**. He then became a professor at McGill University in Montreal, Canada, where he continued his work, most notably with his colleague Frederick Soddy (1877–1956). By 1907, he was world renowned for his knowledge of **alpha** and **beta particles**, which he found at Cambridge. While in Montreal, Rutherford and Soddy also discovered a third form of radioactivity: **gamma rays**. When the University of Manchester offered Rutherford the opportunity to return to England, he eagerly accepted.

At Manchester, Rutherford made plans to direct beams of alpha particles at thin strips of metal foil and measure their **scattering**, or the pattern of their deflections. He expected that the scattering results would shed light on the size, spacing, and perhaps even the shape or internal structure of the atoms in the foil. The first task, which he assigned to his student Hans Geiger (1882–1945), was to devise an instrument that detected and counted alphas. They began their

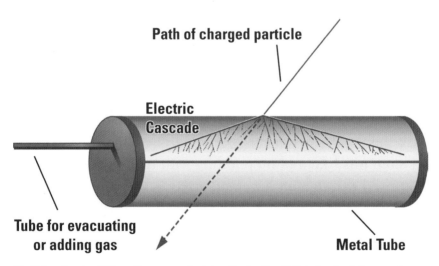

Path of charged particle

Electric Cascade

Tube for evacuating or adding gas

Metal Tube

The Geiger Counter. Still used to measure the intensity of radioactivity today, the Geiger counter (or Geiger-Müller tube) is the descendant of the device Hans Geiger used to count alpha particles in the experiment that discovered the atomic nucleus. Most, but not all, of the air is removed from the tube. When an alpha particle passes through, it knocks electrons loose from atoms. Those electrons do the same to other atoms, causing a pulse of electric current.

Portrait of Ernest Rutherford, 1932. A great scientist and leader of scientists, Rutherford was a pioneer in understanding radioactivity and the subatomic world.

scattering experiments in 1909 and quickly noted that nearly all the alphas passed straight through the foil or deflected only slightly. And that's exactly what they would expect from Thomson's plum pudding atoms, except for one remaining puzzle.

A few alpha particles were unaccounted for. Had those particles scattered beyond the detectors? If so, what was deflecting that small number of alphas so much, while almost all the rest passed nearly straight through the foil? Intrigued, but not wanting to divert Geiger from his detailed measurements, Rutherford decided that the task of looking for large-angle scattering would be good practice for Ernest Marsden (1889–1970), a young student just learning the techniques of research. Marsden found the missing alpha particles. Some went to the left or right of the original detectors, and astonishingly, a few even scattered backward.

By 1911, Rutherford was ready to announce his explanation to the world. He described atoms as miniature solar systems held together by electrical forces instead of gravity. Most of an atom is empty space. Tiny electrons, like planets, have only a small fraction of the system's total mass and orbit a much more massive central body called the nucleus. The nucleus is very compact. Its large mass and positive charge are concentrated in about one ten-thousandth

The Search for the Neutron

Showing that neutrons existed was no easy task. During the 1920s, a number of scientists developed instruments that enabled them to see the paths of subatomic particles. These devices depended on the interactions between the subatomic particles and matter, especially their ability to ionize gases that they passed through. That worked fine for charged particles like protons and alphas, but not neutrons.

Finally in 1932, James Chadwick (1891–1974) one of Rutherford's colleagues at the Cavendish Laboratory, figured out a way to detect neutrons indirectly but convincingly. In 1930, German researcher Walther Bothe (1891–1957) and his student Herbert Becker discovered that bombarding beryllium metal with a beam of alpha particles produced a powerful outward going beam of neutral radiation. They assumed that radiation was gamma rays because of the ease with which they penetrated matter.

Following up, Irene Curie (1897–1956), the daughter of the famous Pierre and Marie Curie, and her husband Frederic Joliot (1900–1958), discovered that the neutral radiation would knock protons out of paraffin wax, which is rich in hydrogen. That was a surprising result for gamma rays, which could knock light electrons loose but had never been observed to eject heavier particles such as protons. When Chadwick heard of that result, he knew right away that the neutral beam had to be composed of neutrons.

Chadwick performed a series of experiments in which he allowed the beam to collide with a variety of gases. By measuring

James Chadwick, Discoverer of the Neutron. This photograph shows Chadwick in 1935, the year he was awarded the Nobel Prize for having discovered the neutron three years earlier.

the scattering of the nuclei of those gas atoms, he was able to measure the mass of the particles in the beam, which turned out to be almost exactly the same mass as a proton. That closed the case: nuclei contained neutrons with the exact properties Rutherford had predicted.

of the diameter of the atom. The emptiness of the atom explains why most alpha particles pass through it with little scattering. Yet on those rare occasions when a fast-moving alpha particle makes a nearly direct hit on a heavy nucleus, the alpha scatters sideways or even backward.

Protons and Neutrons

Is the nucleus a fundamental particle? Rutherford and other scientists thought not. Nature seemed to have a basic unit of electric charge, and so most scientists thought that the nucleus would probably contain as many positive particles, which they called protons, as the atom had electrons.

But looking at the periodic table, they immediately realized things were not quite so simple. The atomic weight of hydrogen is one. Its atomic number is also one. However helium, with atomic number two, has an atomic mass of four. Further up the periodic table, the problem is worse. Lead, for example, has atomic number 82 and atomic mass 207. Protons did not account for even half the mass of most nuclei.

As Rutherford reflected on the situation, he realized that the extra mass might have something to do with another question. Bodies with the same kind of electric charge repel each other, and the force between them becomes much more powerful as they get closer together. Containing so many positively charged protons packed close together, the nucleus would blow itself to bits, or so it seemed. Whatever is giving the nucleus extra mass must also be responsible for holding the nucleus together. Rutherford theorized that the rest of the mass came from electrically neutral particles with masses about the same as protons. He called them neutrons, and he turned out to be right (although they were not detected until 1932).

The discovery of the neutron established the basic atomic structure we now know: a tiny but massive nucleus of positively charged protons and electrically neutral neutrons, occupying only about a ten-thousandth of the atom's diameter, surrounded by light electrons in equal number to the protons. Still, many questions remained about atoms and subatomic particles, including the nature of radioactivity and the powerful nuclear force that binds the nucleus together.

Once again, scientists had reason to believe they had found the fundamental particles of matter. Everything was made of atoms, and atoms consisted of protons, neutrons, and electrons. Scientists thought they would find nothing smaller than those. But in the case of protons and neutrons, they were wrong.

3 DISCOVERING
Quarks

The planetary model of the atom explained Marsden's surprising results, but Rutherford knew that it was not perfect. The biggest problem was with the well-established equations of **electromagnetism**. Those equations showed that an electric charge moving in a curved path would radiate electromagnetic waves—a form of energy that includes light—and it would gradually lose energy. That meant that orbiting electrons would soon spiral into the nucleus, and that would be the end of the atom. So either the model of orbiting electrons was wrong, or the laws of electromagnetism were different for atoms. Which was it?

Clues in the Light

At least two clues to the answer had already emerged. Both lay in phenomena dealing with light. Clue number one came in 1900, when German physicist Max Planck (1858–1947) invented what he thought was a mathematical trick to explain the **spectrum**, or intensity of different colors, in the glow from a hot body. Instead of allowing light energy to come in any amount, like liquid, his formula was based on having tiny energy packets, called quanta (singular: quantum), like grains of sand. When he compared his formula to measured results, it fit surprisingly well. Planck had put an adjustable value into his formula, expecting that it might be different for different temperatures. But, to his astonishment, the same value worked for every temperature. Nature was sending a signal that this value—known today as Planck's constant—was important, but he couldn't figure out why.

A Surprise in the Glow. Hot objects, like this piece of iron being shaped by a blacksmith, glow with a color that depends on the temperature. Its light is not a pure color, but rather contains a spectrum of colors that range from infrared to ultraviolet. Max Planck found a formula that reproduced the measured spectrum, but he needed a mathematical trick to do so.

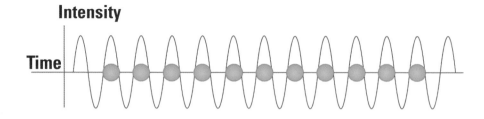

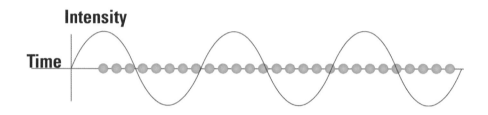

Planck's Quanta. Planck's formula was based on treating light not as a wave but as a stream of particles he called quanta. The higher the frequency of light, the larger the particles had to be. With quanta, his calculated spectrum matched the observed spectrum perfectly. He considered that a mathematical trick, but it turned out that his quanta, which we now call photons, were real.

In 1905, the same year that Albert Einstein described evidence for atoms in Brownian motion, he also wrote that Planck's light quanta (which later came to be known as **photons**) were more than mathematical tricks. The evidence he noted was in a different phenomenon called the **photoelectric effect**, in which light can knock electrons free from a piece of metal. The brightness of the light doesn't matter, only its color (or the frequency of the electromagnetic wave).

Each metal had a different threshold frequency. Below the threshold, the most intense light failed to eject electrons. Above it, the dimmest light could cause an electric current. Einstein knew that the energy of Planck's quanta became larger as the frequency increased. He also knew that it would take a certain amount of energy to eject electrons. If the quanta acted singly instead of in groups, there would be a threshold frequency for photoelectricity—exactly what was observed.

Another clue was in the spectrum of electrically excited gases in a tube (such as the familiar red glow of neon lights). Hot bodies produced continuous spectra; that is, their light would show a band of hues like a rainbow when passed through a glass prism or another instrument that spread out its colors. The spectrum of an electrically excited gas was a series of distinct lines. It contained only certain frequencies and no others. Several scientists had discovered mathematical patterns in the frequencies of the lines in the hydrogen spectrum, but they didn't have an explanation for them.

In 1913, Danish physicist Niels Bohr (1885–1962) put the clues together, modified Rutherford's planetary model of the atom, and sent the science of **physics** down an unexpected path. Bohr proposed that electrons have certain natural orbits, each with its own energy level, in which they would not radiate. Why those natural levels and not others? He looked at Planck's constant and saw that it had the same units as a mechanical quantity known as angular momentum. What if the angular momentum of allowed orbits was a whole number times Planck's constant?

Bohr did the math. He calculated the energy difference between various electron energy levels. He assumed that when an electron drops from one orbit to another with lower energy, the energy difference appears as a quantum of light. That produced a calculated spectrum for hydrogen, and the calculations matched what people had observed. The importance of Bohr's energy levels and Planck's constant were changing what people knew about the subatomic world.

That was the beginning of a new field of physics called **quantum mechanics**. Over the next two decades, many great physicists developed a large body of new mathematics to describe the behavior of matter and energy at the atomic level.

Electrons as Waves

If light, long thought of as a wave phenomenon, could sometimes behave like a stream of particles, could particles such as electrons sometimes behave like waves? In 1924, a French physics student named Louis-Victor de Broglie (1892–1987) explored that question in his doctoral dissertation. His answer was a clear yes. He devised a formula that used Planck's constant to relate an electron's wavelength to its speed, and discovered that the circumference of the allowed orbits in Bohr's theory was a whole number of electron wavelengths.

Now the distinction between particles and waves had blurred completely, and other physicists struggled to find new ways to understand the laws of motion within the atom. Among them was Erwin Schrödinger (1887–1961), who developed an equation that described a particle's position by a mathematical formula called a wave function. Schrödinger's equation launched a new field of physics called quantum mechanics. Strangely, a particle was no longer considered to be in an exact place. Rather, the particle's wave function gave the probability of finding it in many different places.

To understand what that means, imagine an object bouncing back and forth so fast on a very tight spring that all you can see is a blur. Near the ends of its bounces, the object moves more slowly and the blur lessens. So where is the object? It could be anywhere along the path, but it is more likely to be near one of the less blurry ends than in the blurry middle. In quantum mechanics, the blur is the object.

Louis-Victor de Broglie. In his 1924 doctoral dissertation, de Broglie proposed that electrons could be viewed as waves as well as particles.

Discovering Quarks   **33**

Wolfgang Pauli in Hamburg, Germany, 1935. Pauli's exclusion principle solved a long-standing puzzle in chemistry: Why is Mendeleyev's table of the elements periodic?

One significant discovery was a set of four **quantum numbers** that described the "state" of an electron in an atom. The first of these, called the principal quantum number, was the number of electron wavelengths in its orbit (see "Electrons as Waves," pages 32–33). The second, the orbital quantum number, corresponded to the electron's angular momentum, a measure of how fast it was going around the nucleus.

The third quantum number corresponds to the direction of the electron's orbital path. It is called the magnetic quantum number, because a circulating electron is like a tiny electromagnet, creating north and south magnetic poles. Its value specifies the direction in which that subatomic electromagnet's north pole points. The fourth quantum number, called spin, describes the angular momentum of the electron turning on its own axis just as Earth rotates while following its orbit around the sun.

The mathematics of quantum theory also led Austrian-born Swiss professor Wolfgang Pauli (1900–1958) to the conclusion that no two electrons in an atom can have the same set of quantum numbers. This is known as the exclusion principle. Pauli's work led to the understanding that each principal quantum number is like a shell that fills up with a certain number of electrons. Moving along the list of elements from lower to higher atomic numbers, each shell fills and then a new one begins—exactly the repeating pattern that Mendeleyev described. The periodicity of the elements is powerful evidence that the mathematics of quantum theory reveals nature's rules for matter and energy.

The Particle "Zoo"

The successes of quantum mechanics raised questions in other areas of physics. For example, the equations for electricity and magnetism didn't fit the grainy quantum world. So many scientists struggled with a new description of electromagnetism that they called **quantum electrodynamics (QED)**. Although scientists did not have a fully developed theory of QED until the 1940s, they made a good start on it in the 1930s when they recognized that electromagnetic forces were the result of photons being exchanged between electrically charged particles.

But what about the force that held protons and neutrons together in the nucleus? Might that also be the result of an exchange of particles? The nuclear force would have to be more powerful than the electrical repulsion between protons inside the nucleus, but it could not continue to be stronger at larger distances or all nuclei would come together into one giant mass of protons and neutrons. In 1935, Hideki Yukawa (1907–1981) of Japan predicted that the nucleus was held together by exchange particles known today as "pions" with a mass about 250 times that of an electron.

Who Ordered That?

When the general public thinks about physicists, they often imagine brilliant but eccentric people who look at the world from an odd perspective. They imagine Einstein riding his bicycle with his wild hair blowing in the wind. They think about how the theory of relativity and quantum mechanics changed nearly everything science knows about space and time, matter and energy, and waves and particles.

Although most physicists are normal people and serious about their scientific work, many acknowledge that they enjoy being viewed as quick-witted and more than slightly quirky. More than the average person, they seem to love puns, limericks, and inventing clever names. The naming of the quark (see next chapter) is an example of that trait.

Isador Isaac Rabi (1898–1988) certainly fit that image. In his scientific work, he is best known for the discovery and explanation of nuclear magnetic resonance, for which he won the Nobel Prize in 1944. That phenomenon is the basis of the important medical technique of Magnetic Resonance Imaging (MRI). But he is also fondly remembered as a famous wisecrack.

When scientists who were looking for Yukawa's pion in 1937 discovered the muon instead, Rabi's reaction was, "Who ordered that?" Physicists around the world laughed because the remark captured their surprise and delight at an area that no one had ever known about or imagined. The muon opened the door to new research in an entirely new realm of the subatomic world, and they were eager to walk through it. What they discovered on the other side included the quark and the answer to Rabi's question regarding where the muon fit in the subatomic world.

Eccentric Physicists. Physicists are often brilliant but quirky people. Albert Einstein never hesitated to show his humorous side as he did when photographers were taking this picture on his seventy-second birthday, March 14, 1951.

Hideki Yukawa. Yukawa proposed that the strong nuclear force resulted from the exchange of particles called pions between protons and neutrons. Pions were discovered in cosmic rays in 1947, which led to Yukawa's winning the 1949 Nobel Prize in Physics.

The tools for detecting such particles were improving, and scientists began looking for pions in cosmic rays. They also began building machines that could accelerate particles to very high energies and reveal what might come out of particle collisions. In 1937, a particle was discovered that had about the expected mass of Yukawa's pion, but it did not behave in the expected way. It was what we now call a muon and its properties were like those of an oversized electron. Pions were eventually detected in 1947, but in the years that followed, so were many more particles that had not been expected. By the end of the 1950s, a whole "zoo" of subatomic particles had been discovered, and although physicists noticed hints of patterns in their properties, they couldn't figure out a basis for classifying them.

The stage was set for the visionary who—as Mendeleyev did for chemical elements nearly a century earlier—could find a scheme for classifying the subatomic beasts that populated that zoo. That visionary was physicist Murray Gell-Mann (1929–). Gell-Mann arrived on the scene armed with brilliant mathematical insight and an outrageous proposal: Protons, neutrons, and many of the strange particles that were appearing in particle accelerators were not fundamental at all. Instead, he said that they were built from a different set of fundamental sub-subatomic particles called quarks.

The 184-Inch (4.67-Meter) Berkeley Cyclotron in 1956. In the 1950s, this machine was one of the most powerful particle accelerators in the world. Its huge electromagnet guided protons around circular paths of increasing diameter as they gained energy from high voltage twice each revolution before colliding with their target. They eventually achieved an amount of energy as if they had passed through a generator of more than a half-billion volts.

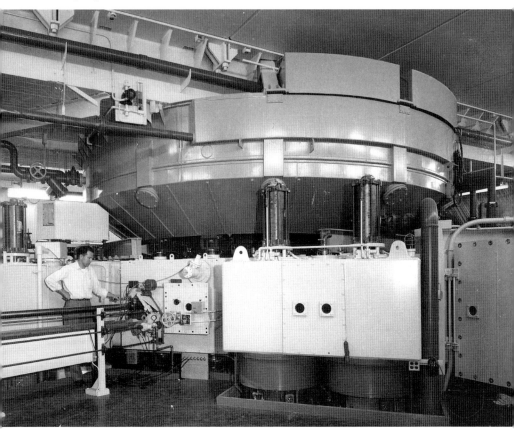

4

QUARKS
and Fundamental
Principles

The history of physics is filled with examples of the search for fundamental principles. This made the growing "particle zoo" both a troubling problem and an opportunity. The subatomic realm was in a similar situation to the chemical elements before the periodic table. There were strong similarities and clear differences among the growing number of subatomic particles, and the scientists who studied them were seeking a way to organize them. Once they found the organization, they would look for the principles that underlie it.

In previous breakthroughs, the fundamental principles often went hand-in-hand with what physicists call conservation laws. For example, the most famous equation of Einstein's theory of relativity, $E = mc^2$, expresses the revolutionary notion that mass (m) and energy (E) are two different aspects of the same quantity (c^2 represents the speed of light multiplied by itself, or squared). Before 1905, physicists spoke of conservation of mass and conservation of energy as separate laws. Einstein's theory, however, changed that in a profound way.

Conservation of mass was one of chemistry's central ideas. Substances undergoing chemical changes may rearrange the bonds between their atoms, but the atoms—and their total mass—remain the same. Conservation of energy was a basic law of thermodynamics, the study of heat and temperature. In the mid–nineteenth century, scientists discovered that heat and mechanical energy were different forms of the same phenomenon, though measured in different units. In every interaction, the form of energy might change but the total amount did not. Now, thanks to that famous equation, mass, like heat, was one more form of energy. And the laws of conservation of mass and energy were combined into one fundamental principle.

Discovering Patterns in the Subatomic World

In 1905, no one had yet detected the transformation of mass into energy, or vice versa. But later work on radioactivity and nuclear physics confirmed that neither mass nor energy was conserved by itself. The new conservation law included mass and energy together, with $E = mc^2$ as the key to doing so. By the mid–twentieth century, physicists had developed devices to show the path of electrically charged subatomic particles and measure their speed. Those devices became important tools, because the more physicists learned from quantum mechanics and relativity, the more reason they had to believe that protons, neutrons, and electrons were not alone in the subatomic universe.

Radioactivity provided hints of one additional particle. When beta particles, which are electrons, are emitted from radioactive nuclei, they have a range of energy from very little to a certain maximum value. All signs pointed to the idea that beta particles result from the transformation of a neutron in a nucleus into a slightly less massive proton plus an electron. Electrical charge is conserved in that event (a neutral particle before and equal positive and negative charges after), but what about energy?

Even when adding up the mass of the proton and electron, there is less mass after the transformation than before. According to $E = mc^2$, that means a certain amount of energy is available for the electron's motion. Though that amount matches the maximum energy of the betas, experiments showed that most betas carry less energy than the maximum. If the law of conservation of energy is correct—and few physicists were willing to consider anything else—where is the rest of the energy?

A related question came up from other conservation laws suggested by quantum mechanics, one being conservation of spin. Electrons, protons, and neutrons all carried the same amount of spin, and physicists expected spin to be conserved in any transformation. Before emitting a beta particle, the neutron had one unit of spin. Afterward, the proton and electron each had one unit of spin. Those could combine to produce two spin units if they were in the same direction or zero spin if they were opposite, but not one unit as needed.

Both puzzles were solved by the theory that each beta particle was accompanied by a **neutrino**, a very light, electrically neutral particle with the same amount of spin as a proton, neutron, or electron. Because neutrinos were uncharged, they were invisible to particle detectors. They also did not interact very much. They therefore could not be detected by their effects on charged particles the way neutrons had been "seen" in Chadwick's work. Still, conservation laws are powerful tools for understanding nature, and therefore most physicists were persuaded that neutrinos were real from the time they were proposed in the early 1930s. They were finally detected in 1956.

Paul Dirac. Dirac is best known for an equation that combined relativity and quantum mechanics. His equation predicted the possibility of antimatter three years before the positron (the antiparticle of the electron) was discovered.

Cosmic rays—high-energy particles that stream to Earth from outer space—had first been observed in 1910. Most cosmic ray particles were familiar nuclei and subatomic particles. But in 1932, positrons—positively charged antimatter versions of electrons—were detected. That discovery came only four years after British physicist Paul Dirac (1902–1984) had developed mathematics combining relativity and quantum mechanics. His equations predicted antimatter, but he dismissed it as a mere curiosity. Positrons showed that his prediction was correct, just as Planck's mathematical prediction of photons was proven to match physical reality.

Mathematics continued to lead particle physicists along interesting roads. Their equations began to reveal symmetries, repetitive patterns among particles (for example, matter and antimatter) and their properties. The pace of discovery was also accelerating. Cosmic rays revealed muons, pions, and

Understanding Quarks

other particles with names based on letters in the Greek and Latin (English) alphabets. Powerful new machines, which bombarded targets with protons or electrons accelerated to higher and higher energies, revealed many other subatomic particles, their transformations, and interactions. Some of the interactions seemed to be obeying conservation laws for properties that had no clear physical significance, including one that Murray Gell-Mann and Japanese physicist Kazuhiko Nishijima (1926–2009) called simply "strangeness."

It was all looking somewhat disorderly, until 1961, when Gell-Mann and amateur physicist Yuval Ne'eman (1925–2006), a colonel in the Israeli army, each recognized a symmetry among the subatomic particles' properties of charge, strangeness, and isotopic spin (another conserved quantity that distinguishes similar particles like protons and neutrons from each other). Gell-Mann realized that the symmetry, known by the mathematical name of SU(3), contained an important refinement in our understanding of matter.

SU(3) led Gell-Mann to propose that protons, neutrons, and many strange particles are not fundamental but are composed of smaller entities that he later called quarks. Those quarks came in three "flavors," designated up, down, and strange. Unlike Planck, who proposed photons but considered them a mathematical convenience, and Dirac, who dismissed antimatter as an oddity of his equations, Gell-Mann insisted that quarks were real. In fact, just as Mendeleyev predicted the properties of missing elements in the periodic table, Gell-Mann and Ne'eman predicted the properties of an undiscovered particle called the omega-minus, which was composed of three strange quarks. When that particle was

High-Energy Particles in a Cloud Chamber. Many of the particles in the particle "zoo" were first detected in a cloud chamber like this one. It reveals the path of a charged particle in much the same way that the passage of an airplane can be detected by its contrail in the sky.

Murray Gell-Mann in 2012. More than fifty years before this photo, Gell-Mann discovered a way to bring order to the particle "zoo." In doing so, he recognized that protons and neutrons were made up of even smaller particles that he called quarks.

detected in 1964, Gell-Mann's confidence in the existence of quarks was vindicated.

Quarks have some very unusual characteristics. All subatomic particles known up to that point had the same fundamental amount of electric charge—one whole unit of either positive or negative electricity. Quarks had a charge of either ⅓ or ⅔ of that amount. The up quark has a charge of +⅔, and both the down and strange quarks have a charge of -⅓. Protons are made of two ups and a down quark, while neutrons are made of two downs and an up quark. The significance of strangeness became clear. It is the number of strange quarks in the particle.

How Do You Pronounce Q-u-a-r-k?

Like most physicists, Murray Gell-Mann is very serious about his work but has a whimsical side. When he came up with the set of three sub-subatomic particles, he decided to give them a funny name. In his biography, *The Quark and the Jaguar*, Gell-Mann writes: "I had the sound first, without the spelling, which could have been 'kwork.'" Later, he decided on its spelling when he discovered the phrase "Three quarks for Muster Mark" while browsing a favorite book, *Finnegan's Wake*, by James Joyce, an Irish author famous for playing with language.

That choice has led to an amusing dispute. Joyce's use of the word quark clearly rhymes with Mark, not pork. So some people insist on pronouncing it that way, despite Gell-Mann's statement that he chose the sound before the spelling.

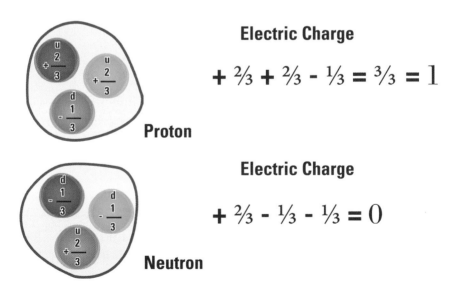

Electric Charge

$$+ \tfrac{2}{3} + \tfrac{2}{3} - \tfrac{1}{3} = \tfrac{3}{3} = 1$$

Proton

Electric Charge

$$+ \tfrac{2}{3} - \tfrac{1}{3} - \tfrac{1}{3} = 0$$

Neutron

Inside Protons and Neutrons. According to Gell-Mann's theory, all particles that respond to the strong force, including protons and neutrons, are made of quarks. Quarks can take on any of three "colors," designated red, green, and blue. Quark color has nothing to do with light. It is more like positive or negative electric charge, except it can take on three values rather than two. If quarks of all three colors are present, the particle is bound tightly together.

Quarks or Aces?

Murray Gell-Mann gets the lion's share of attention for the idea of sub-subatomic particles that make up protons, neutrons, and many other beasts in the particle zoo. But he was not the only physicist to consider the possibility that those particles were not fundamental. In the same year that Gell-Mann published his theory, 1964, George Zweig wrote about a similar model of the subatomic world.

Zweig's theory was based on four particles instead of Gell-Mann's three. Because there are four suits in a deck of cards, he called his proposed fundamental units "aces." Even though his model was ultimately shown to be incorrect in its number, his "spade" work became very valuable in shaping the scientific thought about the "heart" of matter. His ideas were important, and many scientists believe that he deserves a place among Nobel Prize winners.

Although that particular honor has never come his way, Zweig has received significant recognition for his scientific work, first in physics, and later in neurobiology, where he specialized in understanding how structures within the human ear translate sound into nerve impulses that reach the brain's auditory cortex.

Another odd property of quarks is that they always stick together in pairs or triplets and can never be found alone. That is because of the unusual nature of the force between them. That force depends on a property of quarks that physicists have come to call **color**, though it has nothing to do with light. Color plays the same role for quarks that electric charge plays for particles that experience the electromagnetic force.

George Zweig. At the same time Gell-Mann was writing about up, down, and strange quarks, Zweig made a similar proposal about four sub-subatomic particles that he called "aces" since there are four aces in a deck of cards. We now know that subatomic particles include six types of quarks, Gell-Mann's original three plus charm, top, and bottom.

Electric charge comes in two types, positive and negative, but the property of color has three: red, blue, and green. (Antiquarks come in anti-red, anti-blue, and anti-green.) Quarks of different colors attract each other, and quarks of the same color repel each other. Thus a proton, neutron, or any other three-quark particle must have one of each color to stay together. (Pions, which carry the forces between protons and neutrons, are combinations of a quark of a particular color and a different antiquark of the corresponding anti-color.)

Calculating the forces between quarks, Gell-Mann developed a theory similar to quantum electrodynamics, which by then had a well-established mathematical form. He called it **quantum chromodynamics (QCD)**, and based the force between quarks on the exchange of particles called **gluons**. The result was a force that acted as a spring between quarks of different colors, becoming stronger as they get farther apart. That explained why quarks were inseparable, though they could move freely when they are close together.

In the late 1960s and early 1970s, several teams of scientists detected quarks within protons and neutrons by performing an experiment similar to the one in which Rutherford discovered the nucleus. They shot beams of electrons at protons or neutrons and observed the scattering. The protons and neutrons were like sacks containing three jiggling lumps.

Nuclear Forces, Charm, Truth, and Beauty

While Gell-Mann was leading the way to understanding the **strong nuclear force** that held quarks together and also bound protons and neutrons into a nucleus, other researchers were trying to make sense of the **weak nuclear force** that is involved in beta radiation. Neutrons have a tendency to turn into protons while spitting out electrons and neutrinos, but the **weak force** prevents that most of the time, especially within nuclei.

The Elementary Particles of the Standard Model

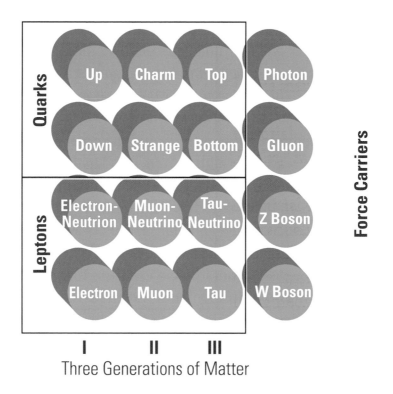

Three Generations of Matter

The Standard Model of Particle Physics. Research has shown that the subatomic world is made up of a small number of subatomic particles that can be arranged in three generations, as shown in this diagram. Each generation contains two quarks and two leptons, one of which is a neutrino. The fundamental forces of nature result from the exchange of bosons between particles. For electromagnetism, the force carrying boson is the photon. For the strong force, it is the gluon. The weak force has three bosons, which include positively and negatively charged Ws and electrically neutral Zs.

In 1970, the team of Sheldon Glashow (1932–), John Iliopoulos (1940–), and Luciano Maiani (1941–) found a way to combine the weak and electromagnetic forces into one. Their theory required a fourth type of quark, which became known as "charm." This theory predicted that a charm quark of one color and an anti-charm quark of the corresponding anti-color might combine into a single particle. In 1974, teams working at large accelerators on opposite coasts of the United States each found the particle. That discovery put all the then-known particles in perspective.

Atoms, as we know them, are made of the so-called first generation of fundamental particles: two quarks (up and down) that respond to the strong nuclear force and make up protons and neutrons, plus two **leptons** that do not respond to the strong force. The leptons are the electron and the renamed electron-neutrino. The reason for adding "electron" to the name of the neutrino was the discovery of a second generation of more massive fundamental particles. That generation consists of two more quarks (strange and charm) plus two more leptons, the muon and the muon-neutrino (discovered in 1962).

In 1975, researchers discovered the first member of a third generation of fundamental particles, an even more oversized version of the electron called a tau particle. Since each generation consisted of two quarks and two leptons, the discovery of the tau led to predictions of two more quarks called bottom (or beauty) and top (or truth), and a tau-neutrino. By 2000, scientists had discovered evidence of all of these.

It is natural to wonder how many more generations of more massive fundamental particles there might be. The evidence, surprisingly, is that three is the limit. Some experiments show that the three neutrinos may, in fact, be the same particle switching among different modes. The idea of mode-switching is supported by measurements of electron neutrinos from the sun, which consistently number only about one-third of what the Sun is expected to produce. Mode switching accounts for the missing neutrinos because the solar neutrinos have enough time to become a random mix of the three neutrino types on the way to Earth.

On the other hand, if there were more than three modes, even more electron-neutrinos would be missing. Thus, particle physicists now think that three generations of quarks and leptons are all that nature has to offer. Still, physicists have had too many surprises in the quest for fundamental particles to close the book. They are still looking for what some call "the theory of everything" that unites all the forces, including gravity and the strong force, just as the electromagnetic and weak force have now been combined. A few ideas have been put forward, but physicists disagree about how well they describe natural phenomena.

To test those ideas, as well as other theories about quarks, leptons, and other particles of the subatomic world, scientists are designing and building even more powerful particle accelerators, which you can read about in *Understanding the Large Hadron Collider* in this series. We have gone beyond atoms, beyond nuclei, and beyond protons and neutrons in the search for what is fundamental in matter. We have found three generations of quarks and leptons, but our 2,500-year-old quest for nature's fundamental particles may not be finished yet!

Glossary

alchemy A predecessor field to chemistry through which many people hoped to transform less valuable metals into gold but never succeeded.

alpha particle A helium nucleus that is emitted from some radioactive elements.

atom The smallest bit of matter than can be identified as a certain chemical element.

atomic mass or **atomic weight** A number that specifies the mass of the atoms of a particular element. For naturally occurring elements, it is approximately equal to the number of protons plus the average number of neutrons in the nuclei.

atomic number The number of protons in the nucleus of an atom, which determines its chemical identity as an element.

beta particle An electron that is emitted from some radioactive elements.

Brownian motion The jiggling motion of a piece of dust or pollen suspended in a fluid; first observed by Robert Brown and eventually shown by Albert Einstein to demonstrate the existence of atoms and molecules.

chemistry The science that studies the properties of matter based on interactions of atoms and molecules.

color In the theory of the strong nuclear force, this term is used to refer to the property that particles have that makes them respond to the force, just as electric charge is a property of particles that makes them respond to electromagnetic forces.

compound A substance made of only one kind of molecule that consists of more than one kind of atom. For example, water (H_2O) is made of molecules that contain two atoms of hydrogen and one atom of oxygen.

electromagnetism A fundamental force of nature, or property of matter and energy, that includes electricity, magnetism, and electromagnetic waves, such as light.

electron A very light subatomic particle (the first to be discovered) that carries negative charge and is responsible for chemical properties of matter.

element A substance made of only one kind of atom.

gamma ray A high-energy photon that is emitted from some radioactive elements.

gluon A particle that is exchanged between quarks, resulting in their being bound together.

lepton A subatomic particle that does not respond to the strong nuclear force. The leptons include electrons, muons, taus, and their corresponding neutrinos.

molecule The smallest bit of matter that can be identified as a certain chemical compound.

neutrino A subatomic particle with very little mass and no electric charge that is emitted along with an electron in beta radiation.

neutron A subatomic particle with neutral electric charge found in the nucleus of atoms.

nucleus The very tiny, positively charged central part of an atom that carries most of its mass.

periodic table of the elements An arrangement of the elements in rows and columns by increasing atomic number in which elements in the same column have similar chemical properties.

photoelectric effect A phenomenon in which light can, under some circumstances, knock electrons out of atoms. Einstein's explanation of this effect led to scientific acceptance of the photon as a particle and eventually to quantum mechanics.

photon A particle that carries electromagnetic energy, such as light energy, originally called a quantum of light.

proton A subatomic particle with positive electric charge found in the nucleus of atoms.

physics The science of matter and energy.

quantum chromodynamics (QCD) A mathematical description of the "color" force between quarks and the resulting strong nuclear force between protons and neutrons.

quantum electrodynamics (QED) A mathematical description of the electromagnetic force that accounts for quantum mechanical phenomena.

quantum mechanics A field of physics developed to describe the relationships between matter and energy that accounts for the dual wave-particle nature of both.

quantum number One of several numbers that specifies the state of a property of a subatomic particle, such as its orbital characteristics within an atom or its spin.

quark A sub-subatomic particle that exists in several forms that combine to make protons, neutrons, and some other subatomic particles.

radioactivity A property of unstable atoms that causes them to emit alpha, beta, or gamma rays.

scattering An experimental technique used to detect the shape or properties of an unseen object by observing how other objects deflect from it.

spectrum (plural spectra) The mixture of colors contained within a beam of light, or the band produced when those colors are spread out by a prism or other device that separates the colors from each other.

strong nuclear force or **strong force** A fundamental force of nature that acts to hold the protons and neutrons in a nucleus together.

theory of relativity a theory developed by Albert Einstein that dealt with the relationship between space and time. Its most famous equation ($E = mc^2$) described the relationship between mass and energy.

weak nuclear force or **weak force** A fundamental force of nature that is responsible for beta decay of a radioactive nucleus.

For Further Information

Books

Bortz, Fred. *The Periodic Table of Elements and Dmitry Mendeleyev*. New York: Rosen, 2014.

Bortz, Fred. *Physics: Decade by Decade*. Twentieth-Century Science. New York: Facts On File, 2007.

Green, Dan, and Simon Basher. *Extreme Physics*. New York: Kingfisher, 2013.

Hagler, Gina. *Discovering Quantum Mechanics*. New York: Rosen, 2015.

Marsico, Katie. *Key Discoveries in Physical Science*. Minneapolis, MN: Lerner Publications, 2015.

Morgan, Sally. *From Greek Atoms to Quarks: Discovering Atoms*. New York: Heinemann Publishing, 2008.

Websites

American Institute of Physics
Center for the History of Physics
www.aip.org/history-programs/physics-history

This website includes several valuable online exhibits from the history of physics, including The Discovery of the Electron and Rutherford's Nuclear World.

The Nobel Foundation Prizes for Physics
www.nobelprize.org/nobel_prizes/physics

Read about past Nobel Prize winners, including J. J. Thomson, Ernest Rutherford, Louis de Broglie, Albert Einstein, and Murray Gell-Mann. Each entry includes quick biographical facts and brief summaries of their award-winning contributions to physics.

The Science Museum (UK)
www.sciencemuseum.org.uk

This website includes the online exhibit Atomic Firsts, which tells the story of J. J. Thomson, Ernest Rutherford, and Thomson's son George Paget Thomson, who also won the Nobel Prize for his experiment that proved the existence of de Broglie's predicted electron waves.

Museums and Institutes

American Institute of Physics
Center for the History of Physics
One Physics Ellipse
College Park, MD 20740
(301) 209-3165
www.aip.org/history-programs/physics-history

The Center for the History of Physics houses a research library, a photo archive, and has created numerous online resources in all areas of physics, including Rutherford's Nuclear World.

**Dmitry Mendeleyev Museum and Archive
of Saint Petersburg State University**
Universitetskaya naberezhnaya, d. 7/9
St. Petersburg 199034
Russia
(812) 328-97-44

Among the collections on display at this museum are artifacts from Mendeleyev's life and work.

Ernest Rutherford Collection
Room 111 Ernest Rutherford Physics Building
McGill University
3600 rue University
Montréal, QC H3A 2T8
Canada
(514) 398-6490
www.mcgill.ca/historicalcollections/departmental/
ernest-rutherford

The collection includes letters, documents, memorabilia, photographs of Rutherford and his colleagues, and other materials relating to Rutherford's work, including the desk he used in his home.

Lederman Science Education Center

Fermilab MS 777
Box 500
Batavia, IL 60510
(630) 840-8258
ed.fnal.gov/lsc/lscvideo/index.shtml

This museum is an outstanding place to discover the science and history of subatomic particles. It is located at the Fermi National Accelerator Laboratory (Fermilab) outside of Chicago.

Ontario Science Centre

770 Don Mills Road
Toronto, ON M3C 1T3
Canada
(416) 696-1000
www.ontariosciencecentre.ca

The Ontario Science Centre is Canada's leading science and technology museum. Its programs and exhibits aim to inspire a lifelong journey of curiosity, discovery, and action to create a better future for the planet.

Index

Gell-Mann, Murray, 39, 45–48, **46**, **47**, **48**, 50
gluon, 50, **51**

lepton, **51**, 52–53

Mendeleyev, Dmitry, 12–14, **15**, 16–17, **34**, 35, 39, 45
molecule, 9, 11–12, **18**, 19

neutrino, 42–43, 50, **51**, 52
neutron, 4, **5**, 24–27, **25**, 35, **38**, 39, 41–43, 45, 50, 53
  composition of, 45–46, **46**, **47**, 48–50, 52
nucleus, 4, **5**, **22**, 23, 25–28, 34–35, 42–43, 50, 53

Pauli, Wolfgang, 34–35, **34**
periodic table of elements, 13–14, **15**, 16–18, 21, 26, **34**, 35, 40, 45
photoelectric effect, 30
photon, 30, **30**, 35, 43, 45, **51**
Planck, Max, 28–30, **29**, **30**, 43, 45
Planck's constant, 29, 31–32
proton, 4, **5**, 24–27, 35, **38**, **39**, 41–42, 45, 49–50, 53
  composition of, 39, 45–46, **46**, **47**, 48–50, 52
physics, 31–32, 35, 40–41, 48, **51**

quantum chromodynamics (QCD), 50
quantum electrodynamics (QED), 35, 50
quantum mechanics, 31–32, 34–36, 41–43, **42**
quantum number, 34–35
quark, 4, **5**, 36, 39, 45–53, **46**, **47**, **49**, **51**

radioactivity, 22, **22**, **23**, 27, 41–42
Rutherford, Ernest, 21–26, **23**, 28, 31, 50

scattering, 22–23, 25–26, 50
spectrum, 29, **29**, **30**, 31
strong force, **47**, **51**, 52–53
strong nuclear force, **38**, 50, 52

theory of relativity, 18, **18**, 36, 40–41, 43, **43**
Thomson, J. J., **20**, 21

weak force, 50–51, **51**, 53
weak nuclear force, 50

Yukawa, Hideki, 35–36, 38, **38**

Zweig, George, 48, **49**

About the Authors

Science educator and consultant **B. H. Fields** has worked behind the scenes in the publishing industry since the mid-1980s, specializing in books and articles on the physical sciences and technology for middle grades.

Award-winning children's author **Fred Bortz** spent the first twenty-five years of his working career as a physicist, gaining experience in fields as varied as nuclear reactor design, automobile engine control systems, and science education. He earned his PhD at Carnegie Mellon University, where he also worked in several research groups from 1979 through 1994. He has been a full-time writer since 1996.